819.154 GUTTE
Gutteridge, Don,
Inundations

Guelph Public Library

Inundations

Inundations

Don Gutteridge

819,154
GUTTE

First Edition

Hidden Brook Press
www.HiddenBrookPress.com
writers@HiddenBrookPress.com

Copyright © 2016 Hidden Brook Press
Copyright © 2016 Don Gutteridge

All rights for poems revert to the author. All rights for book, layout and design remain with Hidden Brook Press. No part of this book may be reproduced except by a reviewer who may quote brief passages in a review. The use of any part of this publication reproduced, transmitted in any form or by any means, electronic, mechanical, photocopied, recorded or otherwise stored in a retrieval system without prior written consent of the publisher is an infringement of the copyright law.

Inundations
by Don Gutteridge

Cover Design – Richard M. Grove
Layout and Design – Richard M. Grove

Typeset in Garamond

Printed and bound in USA
Distributed in USA by Ingram,
Distributed in Canada by Hidden Brook Distribution
See BookManager – http://bookmanager.com/tbm/

Library and Archives Canada Cataloguing in Publication

Gutteridge, Don, 1937-, author
        Inundations / Don Gutteridge. – First edition.

Includes bibliographical references.
ISBN 978-1-927725-40-5 (paperback)

        I. Title.

PS8513.U85I68 2016   C811'.54   C2016-903798-3

3 3281 01865 812 7

For Anne,
again,
with love.

Contents

Part One
Remember When

Part Two
Presently

Part Three
Miscellany

Part One

Remember When

Inundations

My Lake had the girth
of the Seventh Sea and was
as blue as cobalt
in white light, and fathoms
below fish rippled
in their millions and clams
colluded with the salt-free
silt, and when the breeze
tilted wayward,
the wind-wild waves
indicted the grain-dense
shore and gave birth
to inundations of dunes
in their sun-sifted silence.

The Village Within

We all have a village within,
a place where we go
when the world fails us,
the home-ground where every
face is familiar and child-
size, where the streets welcome
our walking and each house
is a variation of our own,
its idiosyncrasies known
and loved just for being
there from the beginning
when our eyes were as wide
as any horizon, when all
was new and unrehearsed:
O the tug of the town
that gave us birth is one
of the sweetest joys we know.

The Point

Dickens would have loved
the Point, the streets bristled
with characters who would've been
at home in *Pickwick*
or *Oliver Twist*: there was
Bob McCord who haunted
the beverage room, closed
the joint every day
at six on the dot and whistled
his way down the main
drag, or Ruby Carr
who rescued rags, combing
the alleys and by-roads
on her barnacled bike
and talking to every tree
she managed to miss,
or Butch McCord who battled
bullies on my behalf
and taught me the meaning of boy-
hood friendship,
or Cap Harness who never
saw a sea-going ship
or the sea but cut the hair
of a whole village between
salty anecdotes,
or Harry Fisher whose yard
overflowed with elderly
stoves and assorted pots
like the maelstrom of his mind
and the memories of gunfire
and bomb-blasts on the Somme,
or Herbie Gilbert
in his tin-pot Lizzie,

honking his ooga-ooga
horn at every second
passer-by just
to say he was alive and thriving,
and there was Pussy Carr,
Rip Kemslie, Long
Tom Shaw and a dozen
other nicknamed
denizens who made
my town a place to grow
up in and have your fancy
tickled and fed.

Ascension

When I was always young
I skated over Leckie's
ice-slick fallow
under a mellowing moon
as if my blades were wings
etching the quickened air
with crazed scrolls and singing
filigrees, till a billowing breeze,
stung to my cheeks, lifted
me up like Elijah to Heaven's
edge, and I sailed
up the dunes of the dark
to the beckoning stars.

Eternity

O what a village
I was born to, where the
sun over First Bush
rises reinvented each
morning, layering its
lacquered light upon
streets fresh from a
hushed night's dreaming,
and I sally forth like a
sea-going Argonaut
for the ells and alleys where roses
grow umbilical on
barn-board fences,
ablaze in rhyming red,
and stiff-trunked trees
are surprised by breezes
breathing serenity, and I am
now Earth's original
cartographer, nosing
amongst the by-ways
and fractured shadow:
foraging for a future
unhorizoned by time
or eternity.

Glint

Shirley McCord dancing
the can-can as if it were France
on grandfather's lawn:
she lifts her legs as high
as the glint in my eye and swings
a deft toe chinward
until a tingle of thigh
peeps free, and praise
the Lord: I am too
far gone to think of
sin and gay Paree.

Absence

When my grandfather died
I wondered how I would live
out the rest of my days
and find him gone from the
workshop or the Saturday
supper table where he listened
to me recount the gun—
slinging shenanigans
from the afternoon's thriller,
as if each word mattered
and I became for a few moments
the story-teller I would soon
choose to become despite
the absence of that loving
ear and my desire
        not to be.

Home Fires

After the Christmas turkey
we gathered in the front room,
cousins and all, and someone
started singing "Keep
the Home Fires Burning"
with dark clouds and silver
linings, the swell of the voice
was loud enough to bring
the boys back home, and joined
soon by booming baritones
and tinsel-tongued sopranos,
and then my grandfather rose
after a pair of cordials
and sang "Sweet Adeline",
solo and so soaringly
his throat throbbed and his Adam's
Apple bobbed like an angler's
cork, but under the melodious
tremoring of his tenor, there lay
something deep
and torqued about to be
released: a yearning no
home fires could put out.

Cry

Our village was as quiet
as the proverbial mouse,
but one summer evening
the spell was broken by a
piercing, uncurbed
cry from Mrs. Bradley's
house, like the yelp of a small
animal trapped and trembling,
it rattled windows all
along Monck Street:
"She must be mad, poor
dear," was the local buzz,
but come next morning
the Missus sat on her front
porch and peered out
at the world, wondering
where she was.

Airborne

Our village had only one
hill but it was Olympian tall
and when the snows came
as they did at the sun's
slouching southward
each Fall, we flung our sleds
headlong down
the hard-packed slope,
gaining just enough
momentum to send us
airborne, riding
high on a sliver of sky,
and slung like galleons gliding
on eddies of air, we were
cantilevered cargo
in frantic flight – until
the Earth steadied herself
and we skidded to a stalwart
halt on the bottomland
below, where we limped back
up the arduous steep,
dragging our sleds behind
us like winded Argonauts.

Gary

Gary was gay when the street
word for him was "queer"
or something more
toxic, like "faggot" or "fairy":
a dear boy with no harm
in him, but one day
his drunken father, sensing
something odd
about his only son,
took the strap to him
and shaved his head bald,
but Gary, fearless,
said nothing to that
and walked about the village
without a hat.

Pleasure

My grandfather at ease
in his Saturday morning
workshop: me
on the floor gazing up
at those humming thumbs
guiding the walnut wedge
through the side-winding blade,
as precise and as loving
as a husband's hands
upon his bright new
bride, and I longed
to see the checkerboard
maze he would fashion
out of these wayward
pieces – for the sheer pleasure
of seeing something
beautiful, made
and offered to me and the
                        world.

Leila

Leila couldn't count
the kids she had on a good
day and there weren't many
of those, what with her husband
who sobered up just
enough to get drunk
again, and a ramshackle
house she scrubbed board
by blistering board because,
though she gave the whole
village something
to feel superior to,
she defied them all
and carried herself
like the dark, Arabic beauty
whose name she bore
with a preternatural pride.

Delight

My Uncle Bob prized
his hand-crafted bird
feeder, but the squirrels prized
it more, purloining
the robin's morning meal,
and every trick or devious
device he dreamed up
in his loneliness failed
to surprise or out-think
the fund of rodent wit,
until the day my Uncle
wrapped a coiled Slinky
around the greased pole
and watched the little beasts
swing and sway in every
direction but up:
so now robins could sit
and feed in the morning sun
that shone brightly on an
elderly man's delight.

Grace

Down the toboggan-run
we raced, propelled
by the gratuitous gravity
of Doidge Park hill,
aching to be airborne,
the wind-chill on our faces,
we clung to one another
as if it were Christmas Eve
every day of the season
and the world, for the time it took
us to careen to the bottom,
gave us a whee-taste
of its grace.

Exit

When I was only six
my mother packed me off
to Sunday School, where we
sang of Jesus and the bountiful
breadth of His love, after which
we were chivvied to the big-
arched church above us
to be silenced by the cleric's
sermon that spoke of Hell
and its ferocious flames
roasting small boys
who had misbehaved, so
I ran as fast as my heathen
legs could carry me
all the way home,
trailing God, Jesus
and the Holy Ghost.

Evensong

Bob and I tuck
ourselves in,
hoping that slumber will
overwhelm us,
while a thousand miles
away another child
lies awake in a manger,
where cattle are struck dumb
in His presence and shepherds
are wild with surprise
and three kings have come
through desert dangers
to bow down with hope
and frankincense before
the Babe who does not cry,
while I remain with eyes
unopen and my brother hums
"In the Sweet By and By."

Ritual

In the Autumn we played out
the yearly ritual:
burning the leaves along
the Monck Street curb,
but first there was the frolicking
in the sweet, bottomless
bed of Manitoba maple
and then the frantic raking
onto the road where flames
took hold and smoke
stood boldly up,
alabaster white and pitched
skyward, until only
the embers remained to remind
us that Autumns pass
away and we all need
something fiery
to remember.

Tag: 1948

When we were just kids
we played squat-tag
on the ledges of the village
war memorial, and gave
no thought, as we skidded
and dodged, to the cryptic names
of battles fought in far-
away places: what was Ypres
or Courcelette to those
too young to have regrets
or the knowledge of war
with its maelstrom of mud
and blood-lust and the crippled
cries of those dying
without lament so that
three boys could play tag
on the town's monument.

Shinny

In the Winter on Saturdays
we played shinny on Foster's
Pond, with hand-me-
down sticks and a borrowed
puck, battered and burred,
and a goalie brandishing a broom,
like Turk Broda in his prime
(not even the catalogue-pads
so tenderly stitched
could undo his pluck)
as we skidded and slewed on the slick
surface in our galumphing
galashes, but we were young
and in the air above us
we could hear the skinny,
high-pitched voice
of Foster Hewitt urging
us on, while the crowd cheered
like Romans for the lions.

Shell

My Dad was as proud as a panjandrum,
performing for the home-town
crowds with a skirr of skate
and an intricacy of dekes, glidings
and whirlwind bursts
of speed that left them all
breathless with applause
and cheers so loud
the Bridge above them shivered
in its rivets: he was living
his dream, an Icarus at the summit
and prince among his fellows,
and who then could have imagined
what war and whiskey could do
to a man, his self-esteem,
and the shrivelled shell
        of his pride.

Thrill

Whenever we wanted a thrill
our parents didn't approve
we would head for Barr's
Billiards, where lingering over
a Pepsi we would edge as close
as possible to the shrouded sanctum
and shiver as we listened to the
sinful click of the cue
ball and the subdued hum
of the profane commentary
from the no-good-nicks
who defied God and the populace
for a game of snooker and the kick
it gave them, and us.

Arbour Day

One sunny day
each Spring we were freed
from the clench of the classroom
and set loose to groom
the school's grounds: we felt
like those first gardeners
in Eden, purifying God's
pastures: hoeing
and raking for the Lord's sake,
who tended the tulips
and roses of Paradise;
we took a perfectionist's pride
in the perseverance of our labour,
and when the day was done
we sang our thanks as one.

Mystery

They called it a girl's game
but every Saturday
after football Tommy
and I joined the sisters
Laur for hopscotch,
chalked on the sidewalk:
we kept an avid eye
on the bare-legged one-
footed antics of Bonnie
and Sharon as they nimbled
from square to square with envious
ease, their skirts a-swirl
around their lissome limbs
and the mystery between them.

Blue

In the swelter of a July day
we dove into the cold
elemental grip of the
Huron lake and swam
as sleek as salmon silvering
a stream, and let our bodies
be emboldened by the
giving up of gravity
as we urged the high waves
to break above us as they did
when the Attawandaron dipped
their faces into the teeming surf,
older than Gitchimanitou
Himself and as blue as a
sweltering July sky.

Stone's Throw

There were seven alcoholics
within a stone's throw
of my house: the wastage
of war or the daily drudgery
of the six-day week
took its toll on the men
we spotted on the streets
teetering home from the Balmoral
or sipping silently in forlorn
kitchens, bereft
of any hope or pride;
we viewed them as something
other than ourselves,
alien adults to be mocked
or pitied but never
encountered, by chance or design,
without the shock of recognition,
the sideways glance
that made them human.

Fuss

"Bob Guthrie has drowned!"
a cry that swept through the village
like the ripe rumour of plague,
and my mother, fearing the worst,
sent me running to the
Slip, where the pulmotor
was still chugging above
the unresuscitated boy,
and I didn't know until later
that at that very moment
my brother Bob glided
into the kitchen and said,
while being joyfully hugged,
"What's all the fuss about?"

Friends

I was terrified of heights
but Butch negotiated
the rigid girders of Blue-
water Bridge with all
the aplomb of a high-wire
wizard, arms out-flung
and tilting with tiny just-
in-time manoeuvres
as he inched tip-toe
over tip-toe along
the unbending steel,
and never once giving
the "Look at me!" sign,
letting me know we were
best friends.

Beyond Words

My Dad was addicted to the booze;
he preferred his whiskey watered
to make it last a little
longer, but he never failed
to smile through his blurred haze
with everything but his eyes,
where all the disappointment
of a lifetime oozed
out at me, and bereft
of the pride he hadn't had
for a dozen years, I heard
him say, "I can lick this,
lad," and I longed for those
rare moments when he snoozed
through the afternoons: all
the hurt finally drained
from a face I loved
beyond words.

Main Street

The map of Michigan Ave
is embossed on my brain
seventy years on:
entering the main drag
I see Kopp's Meat
Market where sausages hung
like twisted intestines
and Butcher John wielded
the cleaver with particular
panache and smiled
while he did it, then on to
Burgess Market with its bursting
bins of sugar and flour,
paper bags that snapped
like tiny thunderclaps
and ice-cream cones
as big as balloons,
then it's the Post Office
where gossips gathered
and reputations died,
then came Harry's Confectionery
where we sipped Pepsis
through softening straws
and gazed at the barber pole
across the road, where Cap
Harness snipped and lied
lavishly about his sea-
going days, and at the end
of the street stood the pool
room, the sanctuary of sharks
and no-good-nicks,

forbidden terrain
we shuddered to contemplate:
I remember them all
with a fondness that seems
to grow stronger with each
year I add to my allotted
number.

Envy

And me at twelve, unable
to swim a stroke, watching
Nancy and Jerry make
elongated leaps with
acrobatic ease from their
improvised diving board
above the village Slip,
fathoms deep and forbidden
terrain, and come up
swimming as deft as dolphins,
Nancy breast-stroking
without a hint of ripple,
Jerry orchestrating the crawl
as if he were Aussie-born
while I was left ashore:
alone and knowing now
what envy was.

Sutures

My grandfather's surgeon
was celebrated all over
town, but he was also
addicted to the drink, and in
the O.R. he sometimes
reached for a tot and found
a scalpel in his fist, and so
it was the man I loved
the most was butchered, his blood
pouring out through the sutures
while his surgeon wondered
where his whiskey was.

Missives

If Butch had another name
I never knew what it was,
even his mother used
that moniker to interrupt
our war-time play,
while his Dad purveyed
chops and joints to a hungry
village who called him just
John, and so on a Sunday-
school morning with the shop
shuttered and closed
Butch and I would sip
Pepsis in our backroom
bunker and glue ration
stamps onto brown booklets,
wondering when the War
would be over and what
the Government would do
with our million glue-licked
missives.

Gender

In the little patch of road
that marked our territory
there was a dearth of both
genders, so the girls
passed the football
(with surprising ease) or helped
us mimic the western
we viewed together on a
Saturday afternoon:
(Hoppy and the Durango Kid
with damsels in distress
waiting for a six-gun
salute), and we boys
teetered and wobbled at
hopscotch or dithered
at double-dutch, amazed
at how the tender sex
could do the fandango with the
whistling ropes, a bare-
legged, hair-raising
blur we watched with very
much a gendered gaze.

Easton

When Easton Burgess
had one sip too
many, the size of our rosy
cones would grow more
rotund and our grocer's
smile would widen to include
even the good burghers
who disapproved of drinking
and other peccadilloes,
but we loved him
anyway, smiling back
with double-dips in hand
and pretending not to notice
the ache in his eyes.

Hollyhocks

Along the village lane
not a stone's throw
from the surging St. Claire
red, pink and purple
hollyhocks hung
low over the barn-board
fences as soft and glowing
as a new bride's tresses
or Goldilock's curls:
so we whiled away
the afternoon hours
fashioning hollyhock
dresses out of upside-
down belled blooms,
and dreaming of nuptials
and pied gowns in some
distant ballroom,
far from any ordinary
village lane.

Night

When the evening grew numinous
we gathered with the alacrity
of bats sheering the near-
darkness with their swerve-and-glide
antic, while underneath
we fanned out from the solitary
lamp along the length
of Monck Street, playing
hide-and-go-seek
below a manic moon,
waiting for the all-free
to summon us back
to that luminous globe
like suicidal moths,
where we huddled before the
slow, slithering onset
of Night.

Endearing

My grandmother never
said, "It's five-thirty";
it was always "Half past
five" or "Quarter to six":
time measured by the quadrants
on the kitchen clock and called
out with such cheering
aplomb; I regret
her passing but even more
the loss of those words
that made her both treasured
and endearing.

Flopsy and Mopsy

At the first nip of autumnal
air, Dad would say
with a wishful wink of the eye,
"Time to go hunting,
lad," and I would abandon
my boyish games and tuck
the twelve-gauge in the crook
of my arm, tight-lipped
as we reconnoitred side
by side at long last;
"Well, it'll be rabbit
stew tonight," he grinned,
but I thought of Peter
and his cottontail sisters
under a greenwood tree,
until we spooked one out of
a brush-pile and Dad
yelled, "Lead him by a foot!"
and as the terrified creature
zigzagged in front of me,
the gun exploded against
my shoulder and the rabbit
carried on, unbloodied;
Dad's gun barked
and I was staring down at a single
unseeing, accusing eye;
I looked over at my father
but did not see him:
there, holding a smoking
gun was Mr. MacGregor
in his guilt-gripped garden.

Part Two

Presently

My Father's Eyes

"You have your father's eyes,"
my mother says, not certain
it's a compliment, but I did not
inherit that Roman nose
nor the high handsomeness
so captivating to women,
nor can I skate like Gretzky,
or a winged Pegasus twisting
defencemen into pretzels,
and my fingers do not fancy
the fine-toothed saw
and its willing ways with wood,
nor can I whistle like Bing
or strum a ukulele's
strings until they sing
like Sinatra, but to no-one's
surprise, I have
      my father's eyes.

Tandem
Valentine's Day 2015

For such a long journey
we travelled in taut tandem,
hand-in-glove: if we
were a song we would be,
in our halcyon years, a jazz
jubilee with Louis
tantalizing the trumpet,
and even now when our music
is diminuendo, we remain
melodious: touched
by tenderness, still
surprised by love.

Shy

For the first girl to notice me

I was always shy
around girls, their beauty
both enticing and alien
I could find no words
to demystify, until
the day you took my hand
with a sly intimacy
and unfurled some-
thing inside me
that lasted a lifetime.

Lilac

When my grandmother died
at the dead end of February,
they had to break the earth
apart with picks to fit
the coffin in, and I felt
I had been forsaken,
for the woman I loved like a
mother had left me with no-one
to turn to in my grief: a world
had ceased but I was still
breathing, uprooted heart
and all, and then that June
I went for a last look
at "our house" and saw there
my grandfather's lilac
bushes licking lavishly
at the Spring light.

Baby Steps

For Katie and Rebecca

Everything you did was
miniature: your thumbs no
bigger than a dwarf's thimble,
your fingers afloat in the easy-
going air, you used them
to manipulate your playthings
with gentle gestures and tiny
nimble tossings to
and fro, nothing grand
or gaudy to interrupt
the joy you felt in such
minute possibilities,
whiling away the infant
hours: yours was everything
Lilliputian except
your mile-wide smiles.

Wild Rose

For Kate

If you were a flower you'd be
a wild rose, rejuvenating
June with your bountiful blooming,
and when the morning breezes
whisper through your leaves, I hear
a voice faintly warning,
"Beware the thorns."

I remember the day of your birth,
you greeted the world feet-
first, as if to say,
"I've landed, I'm me, I'm
no-one else on Earth!"

Old Men

Old men weep
easily: a jolt of joy
taking the heart by surprise
or the image of a boyhood
chum, now dead,
swims surreptitiously
into the mind, and sometimes
it's just a word too
kind or an abrupt hug
from a cherished friend,
but mostly we weep for
ourselves, the tug
of what once was
when we were newly alive
and our world had no end.

Adored

I am staring at this old
photo of my grandsons,
Tim and James (now
emphatically grown
into a world they did not dream),
kneeling on the front seat
of my Ford Tempo: they
smile for the camera and me,
caring only for this moment
when they know they are both
beguiling and adored.

Moya

She was old, blind and deaf
but some spirit, some will
to live deep within
the boldness of her breed,
lingered, as she reconnoitred
for food, sideswiping
chairs and table-legs
in her bountiful begging,
nose ever alert for the
last tidbit left
by a foolish, loving
family, and so I
imagine she had no
regrets when the needle
slipped in and her great
heart was, finally,
stilled.

Touch

For Tom

You move among the animals
at Circle-R-Ranch
with the ease of a young man
at home with himself
and happy to groom and curry
these elderly horses
who have served their time
in the trenches and look now,
after a drudging day of un-
hurried labor, for a loving
hand and the lingering stroke
of fingers through matted manes:
like Orpheus you have the prized
touch to tame and harmonize.

Eons

We called it "our Lake,"
not knowing it was eons
old, when Attawandarons
roamed the dune-strewn
shores and braved the brunt
of its fury in birch-bark,
hand-hewn canoes,
nor did we know that Ojibwa,
sallying seawards,
gazed by chance across
its elliptical expanse, stunned
by its beauty, and here we are
centuries on frolicking
in its relentless rollers,
infinite in our ignorance.

Pluck

For Tim

"Free spirit" does not
capture the elongated
leap you took at life:
you had a boy's reckless
curiosity (we had to plug)
the electrical outlets
to stop you from fingering
them for the sheer fun
of it), you were a terror
in the sandbox, pummelling
my castles with an impish
glee, you drove your plastic
car with all the aplomb
of a dump truck bumping
into walls, door jambs
and me, you rode your Grandma's
vacuum cleaner like a bucking
bronco, your blue eyes
bright with surprise
and perfect pluck, and when
it was time for Raffi's songs
I danced you around
the kitchen floor like a
rambunctious ballerina:
you taught us what it was
to be joyful, to love
the child still in us.

Gone

For My Brother Bob, in Loving Memory

Now that you are gone
I think of all the questions
I meant to ask and never
did, and I stare at these
old photographs
of our shared boyhood
immortalizing the memories
I must muster alone:
the way you hung upon
the words of my stories and brought
them alive in your eyes
that will not brighten again
at my preposterous plots
and characters carrying on –
now that you are gone.

Vim

For Stewart Geddes, In Memoriam

At supper you beguiled us
with stories of the old days:
your Dad the blacksmith
hammering horseshoes
hot enough to make
a fashionable fit
for the gelding's hoof,
or the morning of your birth
when Dr. Stewart braved
a blizzard to usher you
into a waiting world and give
you his name, or your loving
anecdotes about Lorraine
and those songs she'd sung
with such vaudevillian vim —
and when you'd wrung
all the pleasure out of a tale,
you'd flash us a smile:
ninety-four years
        young.

Hoping

When I leave this world
the Earth will continue
to circumnavigate the sun
and I will be remembered
if at all, by those
few who loved me,
and when they too are dead
and gone, I'll no longer
be anybody's memory,
merely a name on the cover
of a book discovered by chance
on the far shelf of some
library: encumbered by dust
and hoping to be read.

Dappled

When I die I want
it to be in the Spring
when the crocus erupts,
tulips tantalize
the sun, my maple's
leafage abruptly
levitates and the hedgerows
are hung with berries ripened
by light, when apple blossoms
blow blizzard-white,
and I may lie in some
dappled shade and dream
of being young.

A Birthday Poem

For Sandy

One summer all
those summers ago
we held hands with shy
defiance and wore out
the walks that linked our houses,
moments that still glow
like a jewelled star
among the many millions;
together we made a memory
out of a teen twosome,
lingering and warm
for the years between.

Gifts

For Katie-Ann and Rebecca

The Lake must seem as wide
as Methuselah's lifespan,
and yet they glide like svelte
sylphs from some newly
minted urn into its blue
glaze: I hold my breath
as they hold theirs
and vanish for a suspended
second before they rise
more radiant than Venus
herself adrift on her sea-
spawned shell – amazed
at the lightness of their being
afloat, and smiling at the old
man on the shore: enthused,
and grateful to the gods
for their gratuitous gifts.

Part Three
Miscellany

Wit

Once more I sit
down to compose,
amazed again at the
limned linkage
between the ink-dark
word and the flush of feeling
induced – the pivot-point
in the poem's truce with truth,
where the reader embarks
on a voyage that will leave him
dazed with knowing: words
are both weapon and wit.

The Game

I'd like to write a poem
to take your breath away,
but words have a will of their own:
once uttered indelible
into the air they will have their say,
and when they are stilled on the page,
stiff and resolute, they may
be read in a dozen different
ways or, playing the guessing
game, remain un-
engaged or merely mute.

Rhymes

In my advancing age
let me still be the one
wrestling with words to wield
the world anew, to send
them dancing on some
distant dais, sylvan
with simile: the page
where all my rhymes ring
true.

Birdsong

Robins hobnobbing
on my lawn with a soundless
strut: then, still
as stone, one ear
cocked for the writhe of an
earthworm under
ground, before the blithe
two-syllabled note:
a burst of birdsong
thrilling the throat.

Lost Light

When our world has withered away
it kindly offers to shut
down our softening sight
and leaves us loitering
in the darkness at the end
of all things, looking
back at the lost light.

Bit

When Adam and Eve delved
in God's garden, tulips
bloomed in the dappled shade
and the grass grew as green
as emeralds under a sky
preternaturally blue,
and the lucky couple
helped themselves
to the fruits of their labor
and all was well and fit
until one of them
against all odds
nursed an appetite for apples,
and bit.

Chime

It's all about the ringing
of rhyme and the crispness
of consonance as they predicate
the patterns of possibility
for the choosing of words and the
mindset of meaning,
and when they chime as one,
they leave us a poem
singing.

Pitch

Working with words all
my life, I remain amazed
at their willfulness, the way
they engage the page
as if they did not flow
from the million syllables
of my mind but moved instead
with their own pace and provenance,
unfazed by my paltry
attempt to twist them into
meaning, they hitch a ride
on the tide of their own intelligence
until they find their way
home in the perfect pitch
of a poem.

September

If September were a woman
she would be as lean and lithe
as an antelope leaping,
her voice as lilting as the
autumnal songs of robins
dreaming of the blithe South,
her hair would be as yellow
as goldenrod or the last
of the black-eyed Susans,
and her smile would mellow
the lacquer of moonlight
over an ink-tinted
lake: she would have no
regrets about Springs
unremembered or the
intimations of Winter's
coming on: content
to be the loving link
between the seasons.

Poised

I pause: pen poised
to execute a poem,
something stirred within
moves me to lay down
a virgin page and begin:
a metaphor unfolds
itself astutely, and I
drown in words.

Silence

For sixty-odd years
I've been a wielder of words,
my pen propelled across
the page, metamorphosing
into three-beat iambics
enmeshed in metaphor
and circulating into sense;
when I can no longer be
a purveyor of poems,
I shall leave it all
to God and silence.

Asperger

'Out there' overwhelms,
it is all speed and fractured
light, colours collide,
grow tangible, voices
veer, hands hover
threatening touch, and in the midst
of it all a chasm of calm
where thought moves at its own
pace and feeling is curled
in its own delight: wanting
so much to reach out
and hug the chaotic world.

Bloom

The wind moves mournfully
over the fields of Flanders
and the gunnery-gutted moon-
scape, where a million men
were made immortal by a war,
their souls still clinging
to the shell-rutted craters,
the winding mud-drenched
trenches, and bayonets abandoned
under a numbed sun
in a place deboned
of foliage and the buddings
of Spring, where birds refuse
to sing in the bomb-blistered
trees – but somehow
when the wind shivers towards
warmth, a blood-red
poppy blooms,
                  alone.

Age

Why is it that as we ache
into our age, the faraway
past looms large
in our daily lives and in
our night-deep dreams
where childhood dramas
play out in technicolour
vivacity and each morning
is a bountiful beginning
to a day that is its own
reason for being, and where
the village tucked between
River and Lake keeps
us from straying off
the edge of everything
and we embrace the Fates
with indestructible innocence?
What else is there
now that we can do nothing
but rage against what
                          awaits?

Le Gros Bill

There wasn't a rink or grand
arena big enough
to diminish the graceful
striding of Jean Beliveau,
who swooped and swerved among
the greats of his day as if
there were only space between
him and the net, where the luckless
goalie had time for a single
blink before the twine twinged –
with all the civility and verve
of a swan taking flight;
he possessed a kind of puck-
wit and stick-savvy
that carried him through
twenty seasons or more,
and a gentleman's mien
that lit up any room
he entered and put a gleam
in the eye of a million fans
mouthing, "He shoots, he scores!"

Cigar Store Indian

When I first saw him,
stiff and posed in front of
the United Cigar Store,
I thought to myself:
he doesn't look like Cochise
or Crazy Horse: this is
a caricature of those
who peopled the woods and plains
with principled pride, whose
sad legacy is to be held
hostage to a twisted history
and the ignorance of all those
who peddle cigars.

Charm

For Anya

You give new meaning
to the word "impish,"
you entertain us
daily with a tail-wagging
delight, your rumpled sheep-
dog grin dis-
arms and your winsome
zest for life reminds
us of our own capacity
for joy and the simple pleasure
of succumbing to a canine's
charm.

Night Fevers

The dark comes down
as sudden as thunder ripping
breeches in the sky,
while I wait for sleep to anaesthetize
and condole, but the under-
tow of the days' dealings
ebbs and flows at the rim
of a dream, impeding reason,
unenhancing hope,
while I quest for breath, feeling
the brush on my brow: the delicate
dance of death.

Timbre

I love the lilt and timbre
of your voice, ever soft
and low, like Cordelia's
in the presence of Lear: hard
to believe we've carried on
ten thousand dialogues
and every word of them
lean and limber.

Caress

My Uncle Tom played
golf from the sinister side
and so did I: we navigated
in tandem the undulant hills
of the Thames Valley links,
stride for stride, while I
watched in avid awe
the enviable arc of this irons
as they feathered the ball utterly
into the air and it landed on the
far green as soft
as a lover's touch, and his putts
were administered with a crisp
caress before they brushed
the bottom of the cup; we shared
a passion and much more
till the day he beat a tennis
ball as if it still mattered
and his heart shattered like a
baffled balloon and there
would be no more affable
drives to sweeten the winds
above the valley of the 'Thames'.

Too Soon

The grandmother I never knew
stares down at me
from the framed photo above
my desk with a penetrating gaze:
I like to believe she's peering
into a future that embraces
both of us: where we two
walk in tender tandem
down a garden path
festooned with hollyhocks
and daisies, until, imbued
with love, one of us
looks up and whispers:
"Too soon...too soon."

Why

In the summertime days
when the sun still flowered
high on the horizon, pouring
honeyed light on our lawn,
Bob and I would hurl
ourselves near-nude
through Grandpa's whirl-i-gig
and its sprightly spray, while
my grandparents sat
on the placid verandah
and showered praise on our
outsized antics,
and O how clever
we were not to ask
why such prized moments
could not last forever.

Saturday Morning

Every Saturday morning
I found myself in grand-
father's workshop,
the stinging perfume of saw-
dust sweetening the air
as I watched the man at the
machine nimble
tiny lozenges of oak
and walnut through the singing
blade into dazzling filigrees
with hands that once cradled
me lovingly in his lap
while he poured intoxicating
tales into my avid ear,
and I wanted nothing more
in this world than to be and be
there every Saturday
        morning.

Indelible

Gerry Mara is dead
and all the willows are
weeping in Gibbon's Park,
their lingering leaves a-droop
like elongated tears in mute
remembrance of our shared
boyhood, enlinked
by that liberating bond
that keeps a friendship
strong and true: we swam
each summer away
at Canatara beach
and played gratuitous games
of shinny on Foster's pond,
slamming our sticks joyfully
on the shimmering ice, glad
to be young, alive and together,
our friendship written
in indelible ink.

Secret Ballot

The Tories who lived in the Point
(some few of them)
were as organized as ants
on a king-sized hill,
and on voting day a sleek
black sedan pulled
up in front of our house
on Alexandra Avenue
and ferried my grandparents
and my parents to the polling place,
where the elders duly voted
Conservative and the other two
uninhibitedly voted
Liberal.

Lou

Dad's pal Lou
loved two things:
fishing and guns. But
his wife put the kibosh
on the latter, and so when he came
calling he pinned his peepers
on my Dad's collection
of rifles safely cribbed
in their cabinet, until one
evening, fully in his cups,
Lou seized a 30.06
and at midnight in our back
yard discharged his prize
gleefully straight into the air,
interrupting the shut-eye
of an entire neighbourhood,
while his laughter could be heard
long after the echo
of the shot had faded away
and we all gave up
guessing where the bullet
had landed.

Abiding

Each Sunday morning
my grandfather would circum-
navigate the village
that held us warm and safe
from the horrors of the war he had
suffered and from which he had
returned with an encumbered
heart and in need of this walking
with its brisk, soldierly strides,
while I skipped along
behind drumming clever
questions as if I were Socrates
interrogating the truth,
and he told me all I needed
to know about the world
except that Sunday walks
were not forever abiding.

Wizard

My Dad was a wizard with wood,
his hands had a wisdom of their own,
going gracefully with the grain:
he fashioned a home for us
brick by loving brick
and a picket fence to make
it look lived in;
I know he was saddened
his son was all-thumbs
and merely an unbecoming
wielder of words, but
I honour his memory the only
way I know how:
with the potency of a poem.

Ambling

Guelph: February 1961

That night the snow
fell as soft as rose
petals on a bride's veil,
and we walked through the
brightening air, hand-
in-glove, our dreams aloft,
while flakes feathered your lashes
and left your eyes aglow,
as if the world were there,
without preamble, to welcome
lovers and their slow, passionate
ambling.